Random Emotions

A Collection of Poems

By. Spencer L. Roston Jr.

Copyright © 2008 by Spencer L. Roston Jr.
Editing by Susie Samuels
Printed by America's Press
Publish & Cover Design by Spencer L. Roston Jr.
ISBN 978-0-615-46246-2

This book is the work of personal views and experiences of the author. The views displayed are that of the author's life and not derived from any person's experiences or views.

Book does contain Adult Language.

Table of Content

Random Emotions

Poems	1
The Author	2
It's Amazing	3
Lost in Life	4
Inner strength	5
Picture, Perfect Life	6
What is Loneliness	7
It's All Gone	8
Pain	9
Anger	10
Being Strong	11
Moments	12
Thinking	13

Love

Life is Nothing without the Essence of the Heart	14
New Roses	15
Robbery	16
Lady	17
This Heart	18
She	19
My First Love	20
Dreams for You	21
How	22
Define Love	23
Unchain Your Heart	24
Dreams	25
Trapped Heart	26
Dear Heart	27
How Can I Tell You I Want You	28
What you Mean to Me	29

A Moonlit Night	30
You are There	31
Beautiful	32
Beautiful Girl	33
A Sight	34
I Miss You	35
Feeling Not Felt	36
First Sight	37
Soft	38
Angel	39
Plum	40
Show Me Your Heart	41
See You Again	42
Compromise	43
Woman Wants	44

Romance

She's Satisfied	45
That Night	46
Sex on My Mind	47
V-Day Night	48
Kissing You	49
Dessert	50
Chocolate	51
Getting Freaky	52

Heartache

Stay the Past	53
Where My Heart Goes	54
I Want	55
I Had to Say	56
Change	57
No More Tears	58-59
Know This When I'm Gone	60-61
Confused	62-63
My 1st Girlfriend	64-65

My Decision	66-67
Questionable	68
Missing You	69
You Say You Call	70
My Words	71
Quiet Thought	72
How Should I Feel	73
Cry in the Dark	74
Are You Selfish	75

Friends & Family

F.F.	76-77
My Purpose	78-79
Sorry Mudear	80
Be Strong Mom	81

Just Me

Away	82
Walking Head Down	83
Walking on the Edge	84
What do I think	85
Colors	86
Questions (pt. 2)	87
Spawn	88
Boy or Man	89
Judgment	90
My Gender	91
What is it?	92
Thinking in My Room	93

Mature or Immature	94
Me Be Me	95
Listen to Me	96
Judge	97
The Dog	98
1 Man Room	99
My Why Question	100
One Bird	101
A Different Person	102
A Word	103
This is ME	104
Me	105
Toy	106
What is Thug?	107-108
Nice Guy	109

Spirituality

I Pray	110
Answers	111
Notice	112
Man in Black	113-114
Make Me A Rock	115

Random Emotions

Poems

Poems are used to show what you feel
Poems are used to show what's in your heart
Poems bring out what's within
Poems show what's on your mind
Poems come from within the body
Poems show your heart, your mind and what you feel
as one.

The Author

It is hard to explain
A thing such as myself
To express my words, my life
In the manner I do
I tell a story
Within a small rhythmic flow
To say what I feel
To say what I think
To speak the words in silence
Of what I want to say
What do you think?
Is what I ask
Looking for the answer
Looking for you to say
I understand

It's Amazing

It's amazing
It's amazing how things go bad
It's amazing how time runs out
It's amazing how things change
It's amazing how you can be chosen
It's amazing how things turn out
It's amazing how
The essence of something makes that something
It's amazing how life can be the way it is
It's amazing how a smile can make or break
It's amazing how we adjust to the changing time
It's amazing how amazing things are but not everyone knows it.
Amazing, hunh?

Lost in Life

*Lost
Missing or gone
It's amazing how you don't think of something until
it's lost
Amazing how important it is when it's gone
Things just disappear
You look at something all day but when you turn your
head,
It's gone
How?
Maybe to learn or for
A lesson to come.
It may be a meaningless loss now
But later it will serve its purpose
Connecting life together again
Life's a string that moves in many directions,
But entwining itself at the same time into one big ball.
Sometimes it flows smoothly, sometimes rough
But never stopping until the ball is complete.*

Inner Strength

My life is in turmoil
I messed up one time and that ignited the flame.
Then problem after problem
The flame grew to a blaze
I can't put it out
But wait until it dies down
So, I wait
But the hard thing for the mind is patience
And not knowing.
It confuses the mind and brings out truth in the inner rage in a person.
How do you control your mind when you're about to lose it?
People will say, look at the reasons to keep your cool.
Think of the people who care about you.
Well, guess what?
It's true.
So, I think about my family, my friends
And all those that just said you can make it.
So, when you embrace this fully and truthfully,
Embrace these words,
You will one day find strength and then you will realize
That was all you needed in the first place.

Picture, Perfect Life

Draw me a picture
A picture of life
A picture of a perfect life
Well, I ask, what is a perfect life?
A life without troubles some might say
But how would you learn without troubles?
Troubles, lessons, and hardships;
The stuff that teaches us to live
To be afraid and not be afraid.
When to be strong and when to be weak.
So, how would that picture look?
It would look blank because there is no perfect life
Or is there?
Think,
What if we all are living the perfect life?
Filled with all the things that our lives should have in it?
Just think, we all just might be already living the perfect life.

What is Loneliness?

What is it when you try?
Let's picture you sitting in a room
Looking up thinking
"I have this many friends.
Where are they?
Why don't they come by and say hello?"
You're in the club
And every time you try to spark up a conversation,
Many dance attempts turned down
And unnoticed by the opposite sex.
Now you're at a gathering, sitting there wondering
Why I'm here
No one wants to talk to me
No one even cares if I was here or not
A picture of a scene.
A scene lived by when you try
But you wonder though all this why people compliment you?
Is any of it true or is life just that mixed up?
What is it?

It's all Gone

Everything is gone
My house, my home.
What will I do and where will I go?
I have no clue
So, what do I do?
I have no money.
Not a nickel or a dime.
I had once upon a time and all I can do is wonder why
Why my house and my home?

Pain

Shedding your blood, your heart into everyone and everything you do.
You don't want to sometimes.
You don't even want to care,
But inside you know.
You know your heart makes you;
It drives you to always, always do what is right.
Not all the time it wins but good wins more.
It hurts you; it breaks your heart to do so much, so much
For others and get pain.

Anger

The amount of darkness inside a person.
To feel the pit of what is evil.
The evil and what you can do with it
You can't control it
It is the most hate, the most ultimate destruction
In these eyes of mine
You see this held back
All the most danger, the most skin curling sight and thoughts
Then you wonder why
How a person can be so nice yet so dangerously out of control
To snap
To have blood boiling inside his veins
That he sees red and thinks nothing
Who is dangerous to others and himself.

Being Strong

Surrounded in a pit of loneliness
In a place you don't want to be
You feel feelings you can't share
You do things to cover the feelings; the emotions
The stuff so bottled up inside
So needed to be let out
But you can't
You're lonely; you're tired
But you still have to be strong
How?

Moments

Looking over an ocean to find an end
An end to the beauty
An end to the cool breezes
But there was none because beauty is everlasting
Beauty is a sky full of natural colors
Beauty is the sound of many small waves crashing into
a flow
But you must listen, you must accept a moment
Because a moment only lasts a moment.

Thinking

How can someone be moved without moving?
How can someone be touched without being touched?
How?
I know examples
Answer these questions
Moved without moving
Acts of love expressed to get love
Touched without being touched
A gift unexpected in nature
Words that go directly to the heart
Examples that the physical is not always the answer

Love

Life is Nothing without the Essence of the Heart

Before you, I wondered why?
Why did I write this quote?
What is its meaning?
I had a few definitions
One that being the main one
Is that,
In life
The essence of your heart of what you are willing to do
Of your true principle
Of your own heart's essence
Gives your life meaning
But this quote
And what it means from me to you
Is that you are my heart which is my meaning
And together will make our essence.

New Roses

Roses are red
As was said
Violets are blue
I want to be with you
Roses are red
Again I've said
Violets are blue because of you
Roses are red
As I've said
Violets are blue
My love is true.

Robbery

Thief, robber, etc.
I call you this because you stole something from me
My heart, my mind and my card
My card you ask
My player card
I was one once but then I met you
With your smile of gold and your hidden heart of silver
My mind you stole
Filling my head with thoughts of you
And ways to make you happy and then happier
My heart you stole with the way you care about me
The way you look at me
The way you are to me
So, to you, Ms. Thief
You stole me
Now I will do my best to be a prize worth taking.

Lady

Lady, your eyes shiny and dark as a moonlit night
Lady, your smell sweet and lovely of a special rose in a spring delight
Lady, your mind as bright as the sun above
Lady, your hair short and soft as a dove
Lady, your skin sweet as a strawberry
Lady, you are beauty and I mean this sincerely.

This Heart

To my heart I follow
With love and care
My heart tells me what to share
This heart of mine brings
A light to which my heart
Follows love; love from my soul
And from my mind
They all sit
In this heart of mine.

She

Searching for a love
Somewhere out there
She is so beautiful
She can talk and listen
She can dance and party
She can also be quiet and shy
She can be funny and enjoyable
She can be friendly and kind
She is there when you are alone
She holds your hand when you feel alone
She is faithful and cannot cheat
She is honest when she has to be
She is crazy with an edge
She is this and more
She is the one I want to hold
Some where she is out there.

My First Love

A screen name is what I had in the beginning
And now I have a voice
A voice
A voice that catches me
That holds me
And my heart
Craving my mind and making it yours
Craving my heart and making it yours
What is this I am feeling?
When I talk to you
When I listen to you
When I hear your laugh
And feel your smile
And I listen and listen
Talk and talk
And I wonder
What is this feeling?
Then you tell me you love me
And I realize what I always felt
Love
So, I love you
And that makes you my first love.

Dreams for You

Did I love you?
No, but I could have
Just like you
I was infatuated but in all
I believe I saw more
I saw what we could be
I saw you happy,
Satisfied and without worry
Worrying about "is he, ain't he"
What he may be doing
Can he be trusted?
Surprising thing is what you're looking for
And what I'm looking for are the same
But you don't see or do you?
Ask yourself
Do you see or are you afraid
But either way it's your choice to take that chance
So, I was patient and remained patient
For you to see a dream
I have of you
Either with me or without but I just hope you reach it.

How

How can I love you?
How can you love me?
How do you look?
How totally do I?
How can you save me?
How without a touch?
How do I love you?
How if I've never before loved?
How are you in my thoughts?
How when I have too many others to think about?
How can you make me smile?
How when you're not around and no voice to hear?
How can I feel your kiss?
How does it come through the wind and touch me?
How when you are so far?
How do these questions get answered?
How about you from you?
So, how can I love you?
How indeed?

Define Love

Love
What is love?
A usual question
But what is it?
Me, I know the essence
Because to me it is not an "it".
To me love is the essence of love
Explanation
Love is when you call just because
Love is the music in that special one's voice
Love is eye contact that never breaks
Love is to sacrifice for that one
This is a sample
A piece of what love is
Or means to me
Weird thing is, you would think I've felt love before.

Unchain Your Heart

Give me your heart
Without question
Without doubt
Show me your love
With your eyes
With your heart
Let me love you
Without worry
Without distrust
Let yourself fall
With you in my arms
And me in your heart
And you in my heart
Will always stay
Let love be love
And us be in it

Dreams

Years and years
This one day goes by
A beautiful day
Where love is shown and expressed
Where people come together
To show their true emotions
And feelings for each other but for me,
This is an experience I would love to show
To have the chance to express something never felt
To do what I have never done
To make that person close
Feel like she wants to feel
Like water flowing softly down a river bed
Like birds flying gracefully through a cool wind
Touch her and make her feel so wonderful
And for her just to be satisfied
And to look at me not saying a word
But look and hold me as if saying
Thank you.

Trapped Heart

How trapped is your heart?
I try and try
To get through
But you hold it hostage
You put it in a box
Guarding it from everyone
Even something good or someone
Why trap your heart
Because of the past
But realize the past doesn't have to be the future
It's when you realize this that you may set your heart
free
And un-trap your heart.

Dear Heart

To my heart,
I give to you
If you were to allow yourself
You would be a dream come true
Beautiful inside and outside
But you hide your inside beauty
But I see
I always saw
You just need to see
I strive to make you happy
I just wish
But not to worry with what I wish
All I do is for you
Whether you see it or not

How Can I Tell You I Want You?

How can I without saying the words?
Fear of what you might say
Of what you might do
How can I let you know?
Without being able to express,
To show you what I feel for you
How can I have you?
But not have you
Not have your eyes,
Your words,
Your heart
Wanting this of you
Wanting to tell you
Hoping you will see it in my eyes
The question I have for you
How can I tell you what
I feel for you?
When my heart can't find the words.

What You Mean To me

In the cold and in the heat
I will make you see what you mean to me
Through the sun and the storm
I will do no harm
From my head and to my knee
I will show you what you mean to me

A Moonlit Night

Sitting in the moonlit night
Wishing you were there with me
I've never seen a beauty so clear
A wonder so beautiful
Beautiful as the sky
O' I hope I don't die
Without holding you near to me but still I sit
Sitting in the moonlit night.

You are There

For every light, you are there.
For every darkness, you are there.
To my soul and out my body
Through the body and from the soul
A feeling I can't help but hold
Thanks to you, new and old
For you there is no cold
Not cold but warmth
The warmness of your love.

Beautiful

Beautiful
That's what you are
To know and be with you
Fills my heart with joy
Being gone does not bring down the thought
The emotion for which I feel for you
Only shows how much you feel for me
To be with a person like myself
Unlike the beautiful creation of you
That is of angels
Heavenly made
That no one, no one
Can compare.

Beautiful Girl

When I look into your eyes
And you look back at me
I get lost in your beauty
Lost in the kisses your soft lips
When you hold my hand
Making me feel wanted
Feeling, feelings never before felt
So, I hold you close
Savoring every kiss
Losing myself in your kissing
Your eyes and touch
Longing for the times
To be with you
To hear you laugh
To listen to the music in your voice
So, when I'm looking into your eyes
I see the most beautiful girl in the world.

A Sight

Your eyes are wide open but closed
Closed to the sight of beauty
Closed from the sight of her
You want so bad,
So much
For that sight
For just a look
A look of beauty
Of the most gorgeous sight
And most beautiful sight of you.

I Miss You

I keep my love truly to you
For you are the one my heart is set on
I think about you every day
When I am gone and without
You always kept my heart and you were always there
I miss you and love you and
You will always have me near

Feeling not Felt

I love you
Words I would so love to say
To speak with the amount of feeling the words hold
To express the most powerful thing
The most ultimate emotion
That a person could feel for someone
I would love to say,
To speak,
To verbalize the words,
The emotions,
The feelings,
To a person.
To have the chance to feel something
That brings care
But also hurt and pain
To have the one emotion that I have never felt
To say, what I have never said
To mean and express the phrase
I love you.

First Sight

Sexy, beautiful, and fine
I'm not gon lie
My thought when I first saw you
Wanting to talk to you
But could find no words
Waiting and hoping for your words to speak to me
Giving me a chance
The chance to meet one of God's angels put here on earth
So, that I may have the chance to be with someone
With whom I hope my words will connect.

Soft

Soft is to feel comfort
Comfort from a sweet kiss
It is also the beauty in her eyes
The silk of her skin
May even be the music in her speech
Makes it difficult not to want to touch,
To kiss,
To feel the most comfort of
Softness

Angel

Beauty from the Man of high
Flown down to me from the sky
Smell of a satin rose
So sweet that nobody knows
Sweet with a certain flare
Cross this one if your dare
The love I hope she'll share
The one that I care to see
From her head and to her knee
You are the one for me

Plum

Eyes deep and beautiful as a midnight's sky
Skin the light brown of a special made color
Lips soft, sweet and made just for the right kisses
Hands with fingertips like
Pillows and heaven to another's hand
Smile that brightens and beautifies
The most darkest and ugliest rooms
Plum is beautiful
Not just beautiful
But down right gorgeous

Show Me Your Heart

Say what you feel
Feel what you say
Words say what you're going to do
Actions tell me the truth
Think before you talk
Don't talk before you think
What you say can hurt
Whether you mean them or not
Where's your love
If I can find it
You're happy
I want you to be
I'll do what I'm suppose to so you can be
But who makes me happy?
Think with your heart
Talk from your heart
Feel through your heart
Or you'll lose your heart

See You Again

You're my angel
To hear your voice gives me joy
To your beautiful face keeps, holds me
I long for the day, that great day
When I can see you again
To hold your hand and maybe kiss yours lips
And hold you close
Thinking these thoughts
Keeps me strong because I know one day
I'll see you again.

Compromise

Let's get serious
For a topic let's say
SEX
My views only
I feel sex is my way to pleasure her
To make her smile
Never stop till she is totally satisfied
Though I may be able to have sex
3....4... times a day
The girl I choose may not
That, I understand
That, I'm cool with because
Everyone's different
But although I may not
Expect sex whenever
I'm in the mood
She should not be selfish
Because if the situation was reversed
I would not
Sometimes she would have to be considerate of my
needs
As I am considerate of hers
So, I will please her on her terms
But every now and then,
Think of mine.

Woman Wants

I can bring the sunshine in your day
I can bring a smile to your face
I can be the one to take you out
The one to wine and dine you
I can give you a dance
Making you feel
Like you're the only one on the floor
I can kiss you so perfect
That will make your mouth wet
And other places too
I can say the words
That will send you to the moon
I can make you cum
Without having to fake it
I can and could but
I am what woman wants
May even be what some may need
But no woman will take the ride
So, I wait
For the one who is ready

Romance

She's Satisfied

"Lay down"
The words I said to you
Kissing your lips
Touching your skin
Caressing you close
Rubbing your hand down your body
Kissing your skin
Your ear
Your shoulder
Your breasts and nipples
Stopping at your belly button
And going back up
Rubbing my fingers inside
Getting you ready
Then
I slide in
Starting slowly, beginning to speed up
I hear your moans
Then become screams
Now you've cum
And I am done

That Night

When I laid you down
There was no frown
Continue with a kiss
And then a touch
You took off your clothes
And then mine
You were gentle and kind
I was the guide
When you said come inside
In and out
Then you came on top
On and on until dawn
Minutes then hours went by
And when we're done and I finish to cum

Sex on My Mind

Sex is on my mind
Imagining you
Your body next to mine
The touch of your hand
On the back of my neck
As we kiss
The grip of your hands
As I penetrate
Your softness
Imagining the smell
Of the room
As I make you moan
As I make you say my name
Imagining your skin
That lovely skin of yours
Soft and beautiful
Glistening with sweat
In the moon's light
Imagining all the things
All the things I can do to you
And I wake up
Out of my day dream
But still
Sex is on my mind

V-day night

It's Valentine's night
You walk into a candlelit house
You look down and find a trail of rose petals
The rose petals lead into the bathroom
In the bathroom you find a note
Saying, "take your clothes off"
As you've just taken your shirt off
You feel a touch, a soft touch assisting you
To remove those clothes
I guide you to the bathtub
And begin to wash every part of your body
And when I'm finished, I pick you up
Carry you into the bedroom
Lay you on a bed of rose petals in the shape of a heart
Then I begin to massage and softly touch every part of
your body
Starting from your head down to your toes and back up
Kissing, touching, and massaging your body
Now it's time
We make love for hours and hours
Till you can no longer hold
You quiver and shout into a relaxing sleep
And this night has come to a beautiful end
With you in my arms

Kissing You

Kissing you is what I want to do
But I have no clue
Should I, should I not
My feelings boiling in a pot
This is in my heart
Doing it wrong might hurt like a dart
Kissing you is all I want to do.

Dessert

Dessert is served
With you and me
And sweets
You're about to find out why I am called
The Candy Man
As you enter the room
You see
A bed for laying
A nightstand with sweets for eating
A CD you hear to set the mood
Along with the lighting
A setting for dessert
You lay down
Then I begin
Starting with the whipped cream of your nipples
Softly my tongue removes and cleans with a little
nibbling too
Next my favorite, strawberry with strawberry syrup
Like the kind they put on top of ice cream
And like ice cream, I lick it off
Your breasts, your stomach and belly button
Finally chocolate syrup and a cherry
Placed on that cherry part of you
And I dig in and dig in until
The sweet milk of your nature arrives and
You have had your dessert

Chocolate

What is sweeter than chocolate
Chocolate with more to offer
Some have nuts and Nugent
Some have just more chocolate
More sweetness to enjoy
With every bite that chocolate
Gets better and better
And you always crave
That chocolate
And what's even better
Is a tall glass
Of chocolate milk
To sip and let
The sweet goodness
Just runs through you
And lay back and enjoy

Getting Freaky

You on top of me
Or me on top of you
On top of a case
Legs all over the place
Touch here and then there
A thrust with care
A thrust in which we share
Up and down
In and out
And like they say
That's what making love is about

Heartache

Stay the Past

They say time heals all wounds
But, does it?
How many times has your past come back and hurt you?
How many times have you been depressed about what?
Coulda,
Woulda,
Or shoulda?
Time is suppose to heal all wounds but really it's you who decides if it will heal or not
It's on you to make the past, the past
For if you don't, it will forever hurt, haunt and depress you

Where My Heart Goes

I ask a question
Where does my heart go?
You ask, what do you mean?
Where does my heart go?
After you have used it for your own games
So, where does it go?
Is it returned only to be used again?
That's what it seems
Taken, used, and thrown away
Only for me to pick it up from the broken heart's trash can
So, is that where my heart go?

I Want

I want to walk in the park
He wants to walk in the dark
I want to talk and listen
He wants to talk but not listen
I want to hold and touch you
He wants to hold and fuck you
I want to be here when you need me
He wants to be there when your girlfriends need him
I want to make love and passionate sex with you
He wants to have sex
I was your happiness from satisfaction
He wants your body for satisfaction.

I Had to Say

In the essence of life
There is heartbreak and heartache
I seem to always be on the receiving end
But what hurts me most,
Is when I bring someone else down too.
It is hard to think that
In saving a person from hurt,
You must hurt them to do it
Why do I have to be the one?
I don't know any other way
But If I did, I probably would not have to
In my poems only the truth is told
That's why I write them
If you could never believe my mouth
You could always believe my hand
So, when I hurt a person
I feel it more because it will hurt me before you
When it hurts you
And forever after you

Change

All my life
All my days
I strive
I strive to be a better man
A good man
For that one woman who would have me
Who would be with me
Who would care for me
As I would love, protect and nourish her
But all my life
And all my days
I have been ridiculed by the opposite sex
Cheated on and used so much
I don't know what's next
I have been dogged by the people who so easily call me
a dog
When I am not
And I believe that today's woman has become the dog
With lies and hypocritical beliefs
I look back and think of a song
Whose lyrics went "you can't trust no man"
Today the song has changed to me.
"You can't trust no woman"

No More Tears

My heart can't hold the tears
So much pain in my life
They dried up
As soon as things get good, they get bad
As if my life was on an up and down roller coaster
Speed down when things get hard
So hard is my life
I say my heart can't hold the tears
To speak as for
No more tears my heart
Can hold
No tears I can cry
For the pain
That present
Itself before me
For the pain
I seem to deserve
For something I've done
For the pain I've caused in someone's life.
For the pain
That seems to never end
For the pain
That brings tears
But for these pains, there are not tears
For they have dried up
On my face and in my heart

Because if they did, I would have tears
To flood rivers
To flood lakes
To flood oceans

Know This When I'm Gone

It's hard
It's so hard
To know that if I were to die
No one would know my heart
So, how do I tell you my heart is full of pain?
Yes, you see my smile
It's a cover or a passing emotion
Not to say I'm a depressed person but I feel pain
Pain knowing what I can do, can be but won't be able
Pain knowing I will satisfy everyone's heart but my
own
Pain knowing no one will fully see my pain.
Pains knowing I can't do or provide to the people I
want.
To look into my brother's eyes and my sisters' eyes.
I know
I know
I love them with all my heart
I love all my family with all my heart
Yet, I didn't know it for a long time
And grew to love others when I didn't know love
I feel there is more to explain to everyone who ask and
asked if I was all right.
No, I never was but you never wanted to hear that
People want to hear only good
Bad makes people feel bad
So, I lie for your benefits only.
That's my heart

I never knew how to really tell a person they're hurting
me inside
Because to me my feelings doesn't matter to anyone
At least that's the way it seems
Now stop for a second
The words are not to make you feel sad or bad for me
Because something may apply to you
These words are only to inform
Because maybe something I would never truly say
Aloud.

Confused

How can I get you to like me?
If I do you right or if I do you wrong
I don't know
I do you right and you don't seem to care
But when he did you wrong, you stayed
I do you right and you barely do anything
If I did you wrong
Would you change?
Would you like me more?
It seems that way
Situations I've been in
Girls get done wrong and care more
But I do you right and you care less
But what if I did you wrong?
Being me, you probably would dump me
Throw me away
I don't want that
But it seems you care more
More if I did you wrong in the beginning
But that's not me
But if I did you right and every girl I'm with, right
Would that leave me alone?
I just want someone I can do right
Not wrong
And her to like me
To be with me

With no debate
So, tell me
If I did you and talked to you wrong
Would you like me more or less?
Dig deep
Deep within yourself
But don't answer
Because it's not me
You're answering
It's you

My 1ˢᵗ Girlfriend

You saw me, before I saw you
You wanted me before I wanted you
But you showed me a sign
Being smart, I caught on and it began
A relationship
You saw first before I did
But it became more
It became a real relationship
Except for one thing
Trust
You trusted me, I thought
But I could not trust you
The things you said, I wanted to trust you
And when I did
When I finally let you in
You dumped me
You threw me to the side
Like the others
So, again I can't trust
But it's not over
Why because now I realize
I have matured in thought for I think
I almost knew
I was falling
Crazy aint it
Falling while trying

No, wanting to trust you
And so now
We are friends
But since that day
That night you let me go
For the first time I feel jealous
Only female I felt this for
But I am mature now
I have grown
Matured so now
And now on I suppress that
And move on
You were my first girlfriend
But now I know you won't be my last.

My Decision

All my life
Well, not all my life
I always prayed
I prayed that the Lord would give me a girlfriend
A girl that I could give my heart to
A girl that's above those
Who always seemed to hurt me
And one day I stopped
Made a realization to myself
That maybe I'm not meant for anyone
Maybe I'm just suppose to be alone
But then, I met you
You, who surprised me
By giving me your number
You, who had and have the most beautiful smile in the world
You, who brought out a smile that I never knew I had
And sadly I messed up
Unsure about my feelings
I was stupid
Changing what might have been meant to be
But in this poem
I want to say I'm sorry
I want to only be with you
In your absence, I tested my emotions and came up short
But with an answer
You are the only one for me

I hope that you feel that you could maybe, just maybe
please
Give this big dumb
Young man a chance
If not, please always remember
That these words are true
And that you're always in my heart
As the only one that I ever
Could see myself falling in love with
So, please always be my friend
But I hope to be more.

Questionable

What am I feeling?
It's not love
Trust me
But do I like you?
You dump me but
In this newly made friendship
The word you said to me
The way I feel when I talk to you
The conversations we have
Having a conversation only in itself
Is new
We can talk and talk for hours
If we were allowed
But you dumped me
Why?
"I don't know how to fall in love with someone
As nice as you, it's not what I'm use to."
But can you now?
But the real question is
Can I fall in love with you?

Missing You

How many people are in this relationship?
Is there you and me
Or just me
When I'm thinking of you
I call
But not every time
Not every moment of the day
Not when you're in my dreams
Because that would bug you
So, I ask, "do you think of me?"
How could I know
You never called
Except for a call back
A call back
So, you only call if I call
And when I talk to you
Asking to be with you
To see you
Excuses, excuses
Every time excuses
But yet you said
"I think highly of you."
Explain the way you feel for me
But you won't visit, call or just…
But you call me your man
But how can I call you my woman
If you're not here for or with me?

You Say You Call

You say I'm good to you
You call me cute, fine and other stuff
You say you can't be with me
You call this best for me
Repeatedly and repeatedly
I've heard this
Why do females (some)
Say one thing and do another
Refuse a good thing
Want something bad
You say I'm a perfect boyfriend
You call me the best one ever
If you are a nice guy
You know this is a lie and
The
"You say, you call"
All too well.

My Words

The words I express to you
Are they true
Or are they false?
Decisions you must make
You must decide
Can one person have these thoughts?
Go through these emotions,
Understand this much
These words,
Or thoughts I put on paper?
They are true
And they are real
I wonder do you,
Do you understand them?

Quiet Thought

If I talk, will you listen?
If I write, will you read?
If I care, will you care?
No true feelings are expressed
In a situation that is quiet
Quiet feelings not being spoken
Quiet thoughts not being said
But still no true feelings are
No feelings are exposed
Why?
Asking these questions for one reason
An answer

How Should I Feel

How the fuck should I feel
You say
I want to be with you
But not in a relationship
How the fuck should I feel
He says
Talk to her
But she doesn't listen
How the fuck should I feel
She says
That girl's not for you
But what girl is
How the fuck should I feel
You say
Don't listen to your mind
But my heart says the same
How the fuck should I feel
I say
I want you
But you say,
Fuck it

Cry in the Dark

Last night
For the first time
I cried myself to sleep
The pain of my life
And the pain I know to come
You laid there in my arms
Asleep
Now knowing this man's crying
I cried cause
I'm not satisfied
I cried because you will not satisfy
My heart, that
Have me crying but why
Why I stay
Maybe I deserve it
My pass coming to haunt me
Why?
Cause I love you
But I cry
Knowing I will cry again.

Are You Selfish

I will satisfy you
I will cater to your every wish if I can
But do you think of me
I don't want you to cater to my every demand
Just satisfy my heart
Every now and then
Make the first move
Instead of waiting
Make love to me
Not only when you're in the mood
Grab my hand and kiss me
Just cause
Show me your words
Are true
I do
When I say I love you
I care for you
I show it
I'm not selfish
And you know it but are you
Ask yourself

Friends & Family

F.F.

Forever friends
You
The essence of what a friend is
Loyalty, respect, honesty
Just words to some people
But to me
Make you
What you mean to me
And what I need in you
A dime a dozen
One out of a million
That's you.
Me
I return to you
What you mean to me
The respect and honesty
That a friendship should have
The special friendship
Which has been created between us
It is unique
It is also beautiful in its own way
We, the essence of friendship
What a friendship should be
Not just me
Or you
But us or we

Together we are strong
Wondering how strong
Maybe strong enough to create life
Out of a broken one
Maybe even to save one
But our friendship is true
To me
To you
Forever
Forever respect, honesty, loyalty
Forever us
Forever friends

My Purpose

The truth
Is what I owe to you
The truth
Is what I will always tell to you
Now and forever
For in this world you are the only
One I could tell
Truth is, you mean more to me
Than I to you
Truth is, I could only feel love
For you
Not to press anything upon you
But that the truth about me
No other person could ever come close
In my eyes
But for you to be with me
Has been a dream
A fantasy of a wish
I made a long time ago
So for you giving me a chance
An opportunity to see
What might be
This gives me a good feeling
Good because a dream might come true

But your words on paper change that
Made me realize
That it was too good
So truthfully the letter hurt
But
I could not get mad
Or angry
How can I when all I want for you is happiness
And from you, all I want is a friend
A best friend
There is almost nothing you can or will do
That will change that
I will always have love for you
Nothing will change that
So, that in my eyes and heart the dream will stay
Subconscious
But I just hope our friendship
Will not change because of my words
Because your words did not change
Nothing for me
Situations come and then they go
So, remember always when I tell you
Friends Forever
I mean it

Sorry Mudear

All my life you took care of me
Looked out for me
But in the beginning I could not see
Eyes too young to realize
The love and affection you gave
But as I got older
I was blinded
Blinded by my own hand
Not able to see
But still
The love and affection you gave
And give
But
Now, I realize I should not look at the cover
I should read the book.

Be Strong Mom

*You are stronger
And if you ever think you're not
Look into the eyes of those who love you
Because your strength is spread into them
Which should always keep you strong
And for my piece, the strength you give me
I say thank you
And I love you
And be strong mom*

Just Me

Away

You in the loneliest place
No friends, no family
No letters or calls
You wish so bad
So bad for a sign
A signal of care
Or just a notice
Or to be known of life
That they are still there
Left here for weeks
Months
Missing and worrying
About people you care about
Friends, family
Or just someone who would write back
Who would call?
But they don't
They leave you
Here
In this place of loneliness
Suffering
But don't worry
Don't think about it
Because they care
And love you

Walking Head Down

I walk with my head down
Why?
Because there is no pride
None in my heart
None in my mind
My head hang low
To show my emotion
The way I feel for myself
Why?
Questions I cannot answer
I look at the ground
Wondering
Why I'm the way I am?
Why do I act the way I act?
Why do I look as ugly as I do?
Oops!!
I answered my question why

Walking on the Edge

Walking on the edge
Where something is pulling me up
And pushing me down
But which is good?
Which is bad?
Is good pulling up
Away from those situations unneeded to experience
Or is it pushing me down
Getting me away
Taking me away from that which is bad?
Or
Is good playing both sides?
Pushing and pulling
Putting my life on the edge
So, I walk this edge
Stabling and worrying
If I'm going to fall
Or, do I need to fall?

What do I think?

What do I think?
I think friend
I think more
What more
But more of a friend
What do I think?
I think of more than just a friend
But only be a friend at heart
What do I think?
I think of caring
I think of feelings
But for a friend
What do I think?
I think misunderstood
I think misheard
But why
What do I think?
I think I feel that
I care for things that can be cared for to a point

Colors

Colors mean nothing to me
Colors are nothing but to see
Colors are destroying each other
Colors are what are stopping us from loving each other
Colors are of sight
Why is the reason we fight?

Questions (pt2)

How can you cry, if you have no more tears?
How can you think, if you have no thoughts?
How can you live, if life won't let you?
How can you say something, before you think it?
How can you push, without using your strength?
How can you walk a path, if it's not meant for you?
How can you know wisdom, if you don't have the experience?
How can you hear it, if it was not said?
How can you show love, if there is none?
How can you feel angry, if you can not show it?
How can you shine, if you have no light?
How can you die, if you are already dead inside?
How can you answer a question, if there is no answer?

Spawn

Whether good or bad
Represents a conflict
Represents choices
The ones that decide
Whether we do bad or do good
I am to get a tattoo
With a picture of spawn but mine will say heaven
For I believe I'm going to heaven but still in conflict
Being human
We struggle to do the right thing
We struggle to make the right decisions
So, I call myself a spawn
A Heaven Spawn
For throughout my struggle
I am good
Will do my best to do that even if I may slip sometimes
But my heart is good and will stay good.

Boy or Man

As a boy, I grew up as a man
A man grown with a mind of old
Older than those of age
They say age accounts your wisdom
But for me, my experience
Accounts for my wisdom
Being wiser than those
That is old
Brings questions
Say that I may not be just
Because the number that says my age is low

Judgment

People judge when they are not suppose to
People judge without
The given power
People judge, why
Because somewhere
In their minds
Jealous, envy, etc.
Come to play
I don't judge
It's not my place
So, why do you think
It's yours
You judge me, but why only by the things
You see now
I might be ragged
Now but that doesn't mean
Ragged later
Clothes are like covers
You have to read pass them for more.

My Gender

Who would shed a tear for me?
When my tears are gone?
Who would cry for me when I cannot express my feelings?
Untaught about life
Only teachings of a light bulb box
Who will see pass the stubborn front and reach to hold?
Without having to be asked?
Who says that because of your gender?
You don't need a touch?
My gender only makes me more reluctant
Reluctant to ask
So, who will hold me when I can't ask?
Who will cry my unnecessary tears?
Tears from only the struggle of my life
To be held
Letting me know that they stand with me in this battle to be strong
Who will?
No one hasn't

What Is It?

Why am I alone?
I don't know
Maybe it's my look
You tell me not
Maybe it's the way I dress
You tell me not
Maybe it's this
Maybe it's that
What the hell is it?
I just don't know
You keep telling me it's not
It's not you
Said to me over and over
But
But it is me
How
I don't know
But something about me got to change
Change the reason
Why I get told this one thing
By you
By you
By you and you
But you all say it's not you
I think it is
You tell me how it's not

Thinking in My Room

Sitting in my room
Again
Again and again
I sit in my room
Wondering what's wrong with me
But is that what I'm wondering
Or wondering why the same thing happen over and over
Alone over and over
Wishing, hoping, praying
Why?
Why wish something not for me?
Why hope things will change?
Why pray for the one thing that hurts?
Hurts
Hurts yet helps
Helps yet hurts
Makes no sense
I know but I hurt
I wish
I pray
I hope
I just think too much

Mature or Immature

How do I feel?
Mature, immature
Young, old
Weak, strong
I just don't know
How am I suppose to feel
Growing up old
To learn how to be young
To be young, old
Or old, young
To me just a mixture
Of what I feel
Young, old
My age not matching maturity
Old, young
Too much being mature instead
Instead of being my age
Mix both and you might have me
Or you might somewhere have wisdom

Me Be Me

Let me be me
Let me care for me
If you won't let me
How can I feel?
Let you be me
Let you care for me
I won't feel it will be you
Years I did not know
Years I did not care about me
But finally when I have
I have to compete to do it
I have to fight to know what I want
Or do I not fight and succumb and who would
I be
No one will ever know.

Listen To Me

To me
Your eyes are open
But selective to what you see
You hear what is said
But not listening
Answer me this
Do you judge?
Before hearing the case?
Do you look at the future considering the past?
How can you listen if you won't let me talk?
If you have a judgment only hearing half the case
When do you look at yourself
And judge?
I ask you
Which mind are you?
Open or selective?
If you're going to listen, act like it
Maybe you need to ask yourself
Am I taking in their point of view
Or am I imposing mine?

Judge

How do you judge me?
Is it by the clothes that I wear?
Or is it by the content of my character?
No, you probably judge me by my clothes
By the dark and quietness of my appearance
Well, do you think you know me?
Do you think I am some type of street thug?
Chosen to speak
No, I'm not
I was the battalion commander of my school
I work with children so they will have a good summer
I pray everyday and come to church when I can
But do you see that?
No
Because you look and won't find out
You see the color black
You see the black clothes
Is that how you judge me?
Does that mean I have no Christianity?
No

The Dog

The dog is of man
Man is of dog
Man can't realize their dog unless they look
Most are bad
Few are good
Why are there not many good?
Why do most do what they do?
Why are good guys being punished for what they do?
Why don't they treat them with the love and respect
they deserve?
Why does the dog live in the man?

1 Man Room

Empty
That's what I see
When I look around
Emptiness, for without me
This room is empty
Loneliness
The only feeling to describe
The pain
In my heart and my soul
Wish,
A begging to not be here
Lonely in emptiness
Wanting someone to talk to me
Whether male or female
Friend or love
Brother or sister
Someone to fill this 1 man room
Or it may be an empty room

My Why Question

Why do I try and always fail in the end?
Why can't I love?
Is it that I'm not suppose to?
Why am I lonely?
Shouldn't I be use to it by now?
Why do I get dumped over and over?
When I treat the girl as right as I can
Why can't I look in the mirror?
Without a bad comment from my heart?
Why do I help, if I know no one can truly help me?
Why don't people see me?
Is it because I can't see me
Why can't I remember my childhood?
Because I didn't really have one
Why can't I complete goals and make a good plan for the future?
Maybe in my heart I don't see one
Why can't you understand me or my words on paper?
It is my words on paper that is from my heart not my mouth
Why do I pray for you, before me?
Because I can care about you before me.

One Bird

Birds of a feather flock together
But what about the one?
The one in the middle
Look as he fly down
With the others
But lands alone
Not that the others don't want to hang
But this bird's different
He can flock or be of one feather
He can hang with the group or he can stand alone
Different yet unique
Being a beautiful word
I try to be unique

A Different Person

In life there are many different people
People who have nice lives
Whether handed to them or
Some worked to have it
But for me
It seems like I can't have a nice life
Can't have the things that please my heart
I feel that I will never feel that happy inside or out
I just feel pain
Pain of providing catering for everyone's needs
I feel like a telephone
Used only to meet other people's satisfaction
Why
I ask over and over
For people
I do this looking for just some love, care or just some attention
But people believe if you work
For it you will achieve it
I use to believe that but now I don't know.

A Word

It hurts
It harms
A word, a statement
That scorns
Not a sin
Not a kin
But just a friend.

This is Me

I will give you all of me
I will give you everything I have
Why?
I like you, I love you, and I just want you
I'll give, I'll be patient because that's me
That's how I am
Reason?
Every woman should be treated
And should feel like a queen
Because they are
Whether they know it or not
So no matter how wrong
How deceived, mislead, done wrong
I am by a woman,
She is still my queen
Fucked up isn't it?

Me

One who is not quick to judge
Who is kind and nice
Always sweet
With poems filled with rhyme
Loves to serve and volunteer
Who is loved as a sweet, little dear
Popular in many ways
Not always in a daze
But a little craz-zy
As you can see
It's only me.

Toy

The Christmas toy
That's what I call myself
A Christmas toy
Something you use
You just play with
Maybe even love
But just for a few days
Maybe a week
Or maybe even months
But sooner or later
I'm tossed to the side
Put away, thrown away
Never to be used again
Until someone get me
And just repeats the process

What is Thug?

You see a thug
Is it because of my skin?
Is it because of my clothes?,
My sagging pants or my large shirt?
Am I a thug because I talk with a slang
Or go by nicknames?
Am I a thug because I wear jeans, not slacks?
Because I wear boots or tennis shoes
Instead of loafers?
Am I a thug because I wear earrings and have tattoos?
And wear gold and platinum chains?
You call me a thug not knowing me
I finished school then went to the military
Got a good job
Never stole from anyone
I say yes ma'am and yes sir
I don't run the streets or pick up hoes
But you call me a thug
You see a thug because of my clothes
Yeah, I know,
I know when you hold your purse tighter in the
elevator
When you check your pocket for your wallet
When you walk in a different
Direction when you see me because you see a thug
When I'm not
Just because you wear this does not mean that's what
you are

Short skirts don't make you a hoe
Wild clothes don't make you a punk
Neon clothes don't make you gay
Talking slang doesn't make you ghetto
I like my style
You may like yours
But don't judge a movie when you've only see the title

Nice Guy

Not the man of female's choice
In a world where bad guys come first
Chosen to be just a friend
Established to be at the end

Guys that are asked for mainly
Under marriage and are driven insanely
You end us with cheating, lying, fooling around
And believe we could take it all.

Spirituality

I Pray

I pray to the Lord
Asking for His forgiveness
Thanking Him for all He has done
In prayer, I talk
When I converse with the Lord
It should be a friendly one
To me, the Lord is Family
Is a Best-friend
As well as my Maker and Creator
That is why I pray
So, I can visit a Friend

Answers

As I look into the sky
Looking and wondering
Asking myself many questions
I realize
I realize that some questions
Can be answered
And some not needed to be answered
And that He has all the answers
You get what you only need
So, next time I look up
I'll say thank you
For He has given me an answer

Notice

Notice the unique color of the sky
Look at the different, beautiful types of flowers
Notice the complex, sweet sound of music
Then look at the awkward way a frown can become
A smile
Creations like these may be everyday
But it is the beauty of it all
The way the sky can look like a wall
But be endless
The way flowers can grow in the worst places
But be elegant
The way a person can feel sad
But be so rejoiced
So, I say notice
Notice the sky
The flowers
That person
Because they were created

Man in Black

I am the man in black
One of God's mysteries
Made into life
Trying to do the right
But doing both
Wrong and right
As a man in black
You may see me as dark
But I am good in black
But a heart that shines
A heart that is good
And that tries
I said
One of God's mysteries
Made into life
I call myself
A mystery
Because as you try
To figure me out
I am too
Being that
I am a mystery to myself
Black
Compatible to everything
And nothing at the same time
Dark at sight

But in darkness
You find your imagination
You find your light
I have light
But in darkness
Not to think of it
As bad
But to think of this as me

Make Me a Rock

Keep me strong in Your name
Give me the road You want me to have
Help keep my head focused
Above ice waters
Let my heart strive to be better in Your Name
Give me the knowledge to do what is right
So I can better strive not to what is wrong
Let me be forgiven for I am human
Let me be greater for I am your child
Be You my Father and Brother and Friend
So I know I'm never alone
Which gives me joy to know
I won't battle alone
For with You and to You
I pray a poem

www.ingramcontent.com/pod-product-compliance
Lightning Source LLC
Chambersburg PA
CBHW060807050426
42449CB00008B/1580